SCHOOL BUS SAFETY:

FUN

RULES

AND

WISDOM

By

Michael F. Coomes, Sr

CONTENTS

FOREWORD

It is my great pleasure to recommend the book, "School Bus Safety: Fun, Rules and Wisdom" by Michael Coomes.

Michael has been employed by the Baldwinsville Central School District, Transportation Department, as a School Bus Driver for over 12 years. For Michael, driving a school bus has been a passion and love far above just a means of employment. He's excelled at all aspects of being a school bus driver with a great emphasis on safety. This passion for safety is reflected in his safety seminars for children and in this book.

Sincerely,

Dana E. Nelson

Assistant Transportation Supervisor
Baldwinsville Central School District
Baldwinsville, New York 13027

PREFACE

As a School Bus Driver for the Baldwinsville Central School District for over 12 years, I have discovered a way to further enhance the teaching of School Bus Safety rules to young students. I have written "School Bus Safety: Fun, Rules and Wisdom" to teach important school bus safety rules to the students and for the students to have fun while learning the rules. Learning these rules can also put their Parents' minds at ease knowing their children are learning proper school bus safety rules.

Children on the school bus are a "Precious Cargo". Teaching proper school bus safety is of the upmost importance. "School Bus Safety: Fun, Rules and Wisdom" is a great asset helping to achieve this endeavor.

Also included are some personal behavior verses such as Character, Kindness and the Golden Rule to round out this book.

SCHOOL BUS DRIVER'S CREED

"A precious TRUST is bestowed upon you, TREASURE it and keep it SAFE."

ACKNOWLEDGEMENTS

Thank you all for your encouragement and support.

DANA E. NELSON
Assistant Transportation Supervisor
Baldwinsville Central School District
Baldwinsville, N.Y. 13027

ALEXANDER F. EWING
Principal, Palmer Elementary School
Baldwinsville, N.Y. 13027

ALLISON BOWDEN
Director, Radisson Nursery School
Baldwinsville, N.Y. 13027

SHARON BOWMAN

LEIGH BRIGGS

AMY & MATT BANKS
Thank you for your help putting this book together.

MICHAEL AND CHRISTINE COOMES
Thank you for all your help and encouragement.

MY GRANDCHILDREN
Kaitlyn, Sarah, Tyler, Michael, Christos and Anna

JUDY COOMES
My beautiful wife,
who inspires me every day to be and do my best.
Thank you for your Encouragement, Patience and Love.

GETTING ON THE BUS

You wake up in the morning,
And get ready for school.
You go out to the bus stop,
Where things are cool.

When the bus stops,
You look Right-Left-Right,
Just to make sure,
Everything's all right.

Then you get on the bus,
With your hand on the rail.
You go to your seat
And you sit down there.

You put your bottom to the bottom.
Your back to the back.
Then you put your backpack,
On your lap.

SCHOOL BUS STAIRS

School bus stairs,
School bus stairs,
You have to be careful
On school bus stairs.

You go up the stairs
And down the stairs too.
Holding the handrail,
As you do.

School bus stairs,
School bus stairs,
You have to be careful,
On school bus stairs.

LOOK UP THE BUS

Look up the bus and down the bus
And up.
To see if any cars
Are coming toward us.

You do this before,
You step off the bus.
Look up the bus and down the bus
And up.

BACKPACKS ON THE LAP

Backpacks. (-Adults)
On the lap. (-Children)
(all clap once)

*Backpacks.
**On the lap.
(all clap once)

*Backpacks.
**On the lap.
*Put your backpacks on your lap.
(all clap 2 times)

*For your safety and your comfort too,
Put your backpacks on your lap.
(all clap 2 times)

*For your safety and your comfort too,
Put your backpacks on your lap.
(all clap 2 times)

*Backpacks.
**On the lap.
(all clap once)

*Backpacks.
**On the lap.
(all clap once)

*Backpacks.
**On the lap.
*Put your backpacks on your lap.
(all clap 2 times)

AT THE BUS STOP WE WAIT FOR THE BUS

At the bus stop we wait for the bus,
Wait for the bus,
Wait for the bus.
At the bus stop we wait for the bus.
We wait along with our friends.

Before we go to the bus we look right-left-right,
Right-Left-Right,
Right-Left-Right.
Before we go to the bus we look right-left-right.
It's the safe thing to do.

We climb the bus stairs holding the rail,
Holding the rail,
Holding the rail.
We climb the bus stairs holding the rail.
Then we go right to our seat.

THERE IS SCHOOL TODAY

Hey. Hey. There is school today.
We'll get on the bus
In a very safe way.
Hey. Hey. There is school today.

We're going to learn
A bunch of things this day.
Take a test or two and do okay.
Hey. Hey. We'll do our best today.

BE CAREFUL AROUND THE BUS

Don't walk behind the bus,
Don't walk behind the bus.
Stay out of that Danger Zone,
Don't walk behind the bus.

Don't be near the side of the bus,
Don't be near the side of the bus.
Stay out of that Danger Zone,
Don't be near the side of the bus.

Don't pick up things near the bus,
Don't pick up things near the bus.
Stay out of that Danger Zone,
Don't pick up things near the bus.

Be careful around the bus,
Be careful around the bus.
Watch out for Danger Zones,
Be careful around the bus.

NEVER SIT SIDEWAYS ON THE BUS

It's early in the morning,
You get on the school bus.
You go to your seat,
Without a fuss.

You are tired this morning,
So when you sit down,
You would like to sit sideways,
Almost lying down.

If the bus stops quick
And you are lying on your seat,
You could end up on the floor,
Smelling others feet!

HOLD THE HANDRAIL

Everybody hold the handrail,
That's what you're supposed to do.
Hold the handrail,
To keep you SAFE, SAFE, SAFE!

When you reach the bottom step
You look Right-Left-Right.
To see if any vehicles
Are in sight.

If there are no cars coming,
You exit the bus.
Holding onto the handrail,
It's a safety must.

Everybody hold the handrail,
That's what you're supposed to do.
Hold the handrail,
To keep you SAFE, SAFE, SAFE!

KEEP YOUR HEAD OFF THE SIDE OF THE BUS

Keep your head off the side of the bus,
That's what you want to do.
Keep your head off the side of the bus,
To keep your head safe too.

The bus will go Bumpitty, Bump, Bump
As buses will do.
Keep your head off the side of the bus,
So your head won't go Bump too.

When you're sitting in your seat,
Take advice from us.
Keep your head off the side of the bus,
A rule that you can trust.

NO YELLING ON THE BUS

We are riding on the bus,
All safe and sound.
Obeying School Bus Safety Rules,
Not messing around.

Suddenly someone yells,
"Hey you" to a friend.
Who is sitting on the bus,
Up in the front end.

The Driver gets distracted,
You can tell.
When someone on the bus,
Begins to yell.

So, when riding on the bus,
Keep your voice down.
Whether on your way to school,
Or homeward bound.

FOLLOW THE BUS DRIVER'S CROSSING SIGNALS

When you get to your bus stop
And you need to safely cross.
Follow the Driver's crossing signals,
The Driver is the boss.

The Driver will cross you safely,
From the signals you will know.
When you pay attention,
You can safely go.

STAY OUT OF THE AISLE

Stay out of the aisle,
And in the Safety Zone.
Doing this is not,
Just for you alone.

Arms, legs, feet and hands,
Should be out of the aisle.
You must stay in your seat,
Be safe all the while.

Other kids should stay,
Out of the aisle too.
For each and every one,
This is a safety rule.

WHILE RIDING ON THE BUS

While riding on the bus,
You want something to do.
You can talk with your friends,
And do some reading too.

Just stay out of the aisle,
Obey Bus Safety Rules.
Keep your hands to yourself,
And keep your voice down too.

EVERYONE WHO RIDES THE BUS TO SCHOOL

Everyone who rides the bus to school,
Each and every school day.
Should know the bus route number
And know the route's way.

Other things you should know
While you are on the move.
You should know Emergency exits,
Your Driver will approve.

Emergency Windows, Emergency Doors,
Roof Hatches too.
These are emergency things
All in place for you.

RIDING HOME ON THE BUS

Riding on the bus,
On my way home from school.
I ride safely,
Observing all the rules.

I studied my school work,
And did the best I could.
Now I'm happy to be home,
In my neighborhood.

HOMEWORK

Homework, Homework,
I've got to do my homework.

Sometimes there's a lot.
Sometimes there's a little.
Once in a while,
It's smack in the middle.

Homework, Homework,
I've got to do my homework.

When you do your homework
And you hand it in,
Knowing you did your best,
You feel proud within.

PAY ATTENTION

Pay attention, Pay attention,
To safety rules on the bus.
Pay attention, Pay attention,
The safety rules you can trust.

Bus rules will keep you safe,
As you are on your way.
Pay attention to the Driver,
Each and every day.

AT THE BUS STOP

You go out to the bus stop early in the morning,
To wait for the bus to come.
You behave yourself as you are waiting,
It will keep you safe and sound.

When the school bus comes to your stop,
You know what you must do.
Look both ways before you go to the bus,
That's a bus safety rule.

BUS STOP SAFETY

While waiting at the bus stop
There is a need,
For you to be observant
As can be.

If you see strangers,
Don't talk to them.
When you get on the bus,
That is when.

You let the Bus Driver,
Know of this person.
The Driver will report this,
That is certain.

WHEN THE BUS GETS TO YOUR STOP

When the bus gets to your stop,
You know what you must do.
Before you get on the bus,
Look both ways you do.

You climb the stairs,
Hold the handrail too.
Be safe as you climb,
That is the thing to do.

Then you go to your seat
And sit right down.
Remember bus safety rules
Will keep you safe and sound.

Hi! Bus Driver

Say, "Hi!" to the Bus Driver,
The Driver is our friend.
The Driver will keep us safe,
time and again.

We will learn safety rules,
While riding on the bus.
Behaving is what we'll do,
And not make a fuss.

RESPECT THE BUS DRIVER

Bus Drivers are in charge of the buses,
Caring for everyone's safety.
Safety is Job Number One,
And it's taken seriously.

Respect the Drivers,
And all they know.
Keeping kids safe,
Is the job they do.

FOLLOWING SAFETY RULES WHILE GETTING ON THE BUS

When you get on the bus
And go to your seat,
Observe Bus Safety rules,
They can't be beat!

The safety rules
Will keep you safe.
Following them
Is a "piece of cake."

NO CUSSING ON THE BUS

Talking with your friends,
While riding on the bus.
You can have a great time,
There's no need to cuss.

Cussing on the bus is bad,
Not a thing to do.
Have fun talking with your friends
And keep the language cool.

FOOD, DRINK, CANDY, GUM

Food, drink, candy, gum,
I wish I could have some.
But when I'm riding on the bus,
I know I can have none!

All these things you should know,
Are against Bus Safety Rules.
In your throat something might get stuck
And that would not be cool.

KEEP THE BUS CLEAN

On your ride home from school,
What do you see?
There's junk on the floor,
And paper...Really?!

The bus was clean this morning,
When we rode it to school.
Kids throw things near the door,
And on the floor...not good!

When you ride the bus,
Do the best you can
To keep the bus clean.
Now, that's a great plan!

KEEP THE AISLE CLEAR

When you are on the bus,
To do this is a snap.
Keep your stuff out of the aisle,
Put them on your lap.

Stuff in the bus aisle,
Is a safety hazard there.
Let us work together,
To keep the aisle clear.

DON'T BE A LITTERBUG

Don't be a Litterbug,
On the school bus.
Don't throw paper on the floor,
Or any other stuff.

When you're riding on the bus,
No garbage on the floor.
You know it should be clean,
As you're walking out the door.

WALK TO THE SCHOOL BUS

When school is over,
At the end of the day.
You go out to the School Bus,
In a safe way.

You never run, you always walk,
You know that it is true.
When going out to the bus,
It's the safe thing to do.

DANGER ZONES!

Danger Zones! Danger Zones!
Have to keep away from Danger Zones!

There are places 'round the bus,
Where you don't want to be.
We have to keep,
Away from these.

Danger Zones! Danger Zones!
Have to keep away from Danger Zones!

STAY AWAY FROM DANGER ZONES
(Dropping something near the bus.)

When you are at school,
Waiting to get on the bus,
Stay away from Danger Zones.
It's a definite must.

If you drop anything
Close to the bus,
Let an adult get it for you
And do not make a fuss.

Never get too near the bus
To get anything.
Stay away from that Danger Zone.
It's a safety thing.

AT SCHOOL TODAY

We are at school today.
Oh! The things that we'll learn.
We will be doing just fine,
No need for any concern.

Math, English, Social Studies,
On tasks we put our mind.
We will succeed at any of these.
I say "Bring 'em on!"

WE'RE GOING TO HAVE A TEST

Here I am in school,
Sitting at my desk.
The Teacher's handing papers out,
We're going to have a test.

I studied really hard
And will do my very best.
I will take this test and treat it,
Like it's a contest.

GYM CLASS

We are having Gym class today,
We're going to have some fun.
Play baseball, football, volley ball,
No matter, they're all fun!

We will get the exercise that we need,
To keep us moving on.
Our bodies will be in tune today,
Just like a cool rock song!

CHOICES

When you are in school,
There's a lot of things to do.
Making good choices,
Is the best thing you can do.

Being honest with your friends,
A great choice for you.
Following the Golden Rule,
Is important too.

There are many choices,
As you probably know.
Make sure the choices that you choose,
Are ones that work out well.

CHARACTER

What do great people have,
That we can have too?
Character is what they have,
In life it carries them through.

Character is who we are,
How we act towards others.
Character is being fair and considerate,
In life that really matters.

.

APPRECIATION

When someone does something nice for you,
And makes you feel good too,
You want them to know you appreciate
What they did for you.

Appreciation is a term we use
To let people know,
For an action or a kindly deed,
We're truly grateful.

LISTEN

Listen to your teacher,
Listen to your friends.
Listen in school,
Until the school day ends.

Listen to the Driver,
On the school bus.
Listen to the Safety Rules,
The rules take care of us.

SHARING

Sharing is a wonderful thing,
Makes people feel real good.
They appreciate the things you do
And makes you feel good too.

Sharing is something that means a lot
And is fun to do.
Sharing is a helping thing,
It's like the Golden Rule.

RESPECT

When you treat people right,
They'll do the same to you.
It is a thing called Respect,
It's something you should do.

At home or in school,
You practice this fine rule.
Respect other people,
They will respect you too.

THE GOLDEN RULE

The Golden Rule is a wonderful thing,
That everyone should use.
It creates happiness,
In things that people do.

When you are in school,
Heading to your class,
Practice the Golden Rule.
Make friendships that will last.

KINDNESS

Everyone loves a person,
Who is full of kindness.
It comes from a thing called love,
And treasured in the highest.

If you're lucky enough
To have this wonderful trait,
And you share it with your friends,
Your life will be first rate.

HONESTY

Honesty is a precious thing,
This is certainly true.
Honest people get respect,
Day in and day out too.

If you are an honest person,
And do not tell lies,
You will be liked and respected
All of your life.

STUDENTS ON THE BUS

25 students on the bus,
25 on the bus.
We come to a Bus Stop,
One student gets off,
24 students left on the bus.

24 students on the bus...

(keep going until no students are left on the bus)

Made in the USA
Columbia, SC
21 March 2018